CREATION,
EVOLUTION, AND
INTELLIGENT DESIGN

CHRISTIAN ANSWERS TO HARD QUESTIONS

Christian Interpretations of Genesis 1

Christianity and the Role of Philosophy

Creation, Evolution, and Intelligent Design

The Morality of God in the Old Testament

Should You Believe in God?

Was Jesus Really Born of a Virgin?

Peter A. Lillback and Steven T. Huff, Series Editors

CREATION,
EVOLUTION, AND
INTELLIGENT DESIGN

GUILLERMO GONZALEZ AND JAY W. RICHARDS

WESTMINSTER SEMINARY PRESS

PHILADELPHIA, PENNSYLVANIA

P&R PUBLISHING
P.O. BOX 817 • PHILLIPSBURG • NEW JERSEY 08865-0817

Westminster Seminary Press, LLC, a Pennsylvania Limited Liability Company, is a wholly owned subsidiary of Westminster Theological Seminary.

This work is a co-publication between P&R Publishing and Westminster Seminary Press, LLC.

ISBN: 978-1-59638-683-9 (pbk)

Printed in the United States of America

Library of Congress Cataloging-in-Publication Data

Gonzalez, Guillermo, 1963-
 Creation, evolution, and intelligent design / Guillermo Gonzalez and Jay W. Richards.
     pages cm. -- (Apologia series)
 Includes bibliographical references.
 ISBN 978-1-59638-683-9 (pbk.)
     1. Creationism. 2. Creation. 3. Evolution (Biology) 4. Intelligent design (Teleology) I. Richards, Jay Wesley, 1967- II. Title.
 BS651.G763 2013
 231.7'652--dc23

                                    2013011724

ON THE FIRST DAY OF CLASS, a college biology professor says to his students, "Evolution is a fact, fact, fact. Get over it!" as he pounds his fist on his podium. Sadly, this is not a scene from a bad play. It is a reality repeated in classrooms around the world—and not only in biology departments. A bright student will understand that the professor is saying a lot more than his words alone suggest. He probably means something like this: "You need to accept that modern science has disproved your outdated beliefs about God creating the world. If you're going to get ahead—or pass this class—you must either abandon your faith or make it fit with science."

If you were a student in this situation, what would you do? You might worry that your faith and good science are at odds. That's not true, but the truth is complicated. We'll try to simplify it in this booklet, and give you what you need if you ever find yourself dealing with this podium-pounding professor.

CREATION AND CREATIONISM

In some form, creation-evolution debates have been going on since before Charles Darwin published *The Origin of Species* in 1859. Recently, an old idea with a new label called *intelligent design* has joined the fracas. If you ask twenty people to define the three terms in the title of this booklet, you might get twenty different answers. Unfortunately, debates on all three topics can generate more heat than light, especially when the combatants argue past each other. If we want more light and less heat, the first order of business is to make some distinctions and define the words carefully. When we do that, we discover that while Christian faith conflicts with an idea often confused with science, it does not conflict with the real evidence of science. That idea, called *naturalism* or *materialism*, treats the material universe rather than God as the fundamental reality. We should always distinguish natural science from natural*ism*.

Let's also define *creation*, *evolution*, and *intelligent design*. Unfortunately, debates on these subjects rarely deal with *creation* per se, but with *creationism*, which usually is a term of abuse. According to popular understanding, creationists believe—based on their interpretation of Genesis 1—that God created the universe and everything in it in six twenty-four-hour days, no longer than ten thousand years ago. They also believe that God directly created living things more or less in the current forms. This is often called *young-earth creationism*.

But many Christians who call themselves creationists believe that a faithful reading of Genesis allows for a much older universe and that God's "days" in Genesis 1 aren't plain old twenty-four-hour earth days. After all, the text doesn't say just what kinds of days are being referred to, or how long they lasted. In fact, since the sun and moon don't show up until day 4, and day 7 doesn't end, the text suggests that these are not the days we experience, well, every day.

Most of these old-earth creationists believe the evidence points to an ancient Earth and universe, and suspect that Adam and Eve were created more than ten thousand years ago. Although Genesis 1 is simple enough for a child to grasp some of its meaning, its subtlety is boundless. So it's no surprise that there are a dozen ways to interpret the text—without explaining it away. These include the gap theory, the day-age theory, analogical days, literary framework, days of proclamation, calendar days, and so on. We don't have the space to explore all these options here. We mention them only because popular accounts of "creationism" rarely mention this variety of views among Christians, who all agree that God created the world.

Christians affirm the doctrine of creation every time we say the Apostles' Creed. Its opening line is: "I believe in God the Father Almighty, Maker of heaven and earth." That simple twelve-word sentence packs quite a punch. In the Bible, *heaven and earth* is an expression that means "everything other than God." So when we say that God is the Creator, we're saying that everything other than God exists because God freely chose to create it. He could have created a different world or even no world at all. Since God created everything, that means he didn't need to use anything to create the world. He didn't find some cosmic Lego pieces lying around. He created without using anything else. Theologians call this idea creation *ex nihilo*—creation from nothing.

If God created everything without using anything outside himself, then that means that God doesn't depend on the universe (or anything else) in order to exist. He is *transcendent*.

At the same time, according to the Bible and the Christian tradition, God didn't just get things started and then leave the creation to run on its own, like a watchmaker who can fashion a self-winding watch. He's more like a master gardener who creates his own soil, seeds, sun, and rain, or a violin player who creates his own violin. God freely and lovingly conserves and interacts in and with the world he has made. Sometimes he does so directly. He calls Abraham and Moses. He protects the Hebrews from the Egyptians, and sends manna from heaven. He even enters directly into history, causing Mary to conceive and bear the child Jesus—who is God himself.

But God is not stingy with his gifts. He gives his creation certain powers. As Thomas Aquinas once said, God "grants even to creatures the dignity of causality." Even when creatures act, they aren't acting on their own. God is acting indirectly through these so-called secondary causes, such as physical laws like grav-ity or the choices of human beings.

At every moment of every day, God oversees his entire cre-ation, even as he allows his creatures the freedom appropriate to their stations. The Bible says that not one sparrow falls to the ground without our Father in heaven knowing it. And even the hairs on our heads are numbered.

The world is fallen because of sin. As a result, many bad things happen. And yet everything still happens for a reason—even if we don't know what that reason is. *Nothing* that happens is purposeless.

BEFORE WE MOVE ON

+ What is the difference between natural science and naturalism?
+ What beliefs do all creationists hold in common? Where might they reasonably differ?
+ How does creation *ex nihilo* show God to be transcendent? How does God interact with his creation?

EVOLUTION

Now we have some handle on both creationism and the doc-trine of creation. What about *evolution*? This term is even more slippery. There are at least half a dozen meanings of *evolution* floating around. Sometimes without warning a speaker will switch meanings in midsentence! Such sleight-of-hand can lure the unwary listener into accepting a conclusion that he might otherwise reject.

If someone asks whether you "believe in evolution," the best answer is usually: "What do you mean by *evolution*?"

In its most general use, *evolution* just means "change over time." Thus, astronomers can talk about stellar evolution, anthro-

8

pologists about societal evolution, and car aficionados about Mustang evolution. Of course no one denies that things change over time.

But in biology, *evolution* is often used to mean not mere change over time, but *Darwinian* evolution, which itself refers to several different things. Darwin proposed a process that, he thought, could make living things appear designed but without a designer. His basic idea is this. Living things inherit their traits from their ancestors. Not every member of a species is exactly the same. Some have traits that make them more "fit"—that give them a survival advantage over others in their population.

For instance, some cheetahs may run faster than others, so they tend to survive longer and leave more offspring behind. Gradually, their offspring will fill the population, leading to faster-running cheetahs. In this way, Darwin supposed that, given enough time, barely perceptible changes in the running speed of cheetahs, or the sizes and shapes of bird beaks, could explain how new species of cheetahs and birds arise. In fact, Darwin thought that when extrapolated to millions of generations, this process of *natural selection working on random variations* could even explain the origin of birds from their nonbird ancestors.

In the twentieth century, the origin of these random variations came to be identified with random mutations in DNA. (DNA is an information-bearing molecule inside cells.) Mutations in the DNA would lead to different traits in organisms, some of which would give those organisms a survival advantage. This, in a nutshell, is the "standard" version of biological evolution, called *Neo-Darwinism*. (We'll just refer to *Darwinism* in the following discussion.)

Mutations are accidents caused by radiation events or errors in chemistry that alter genes. Some of these errors will give an organism a survival advantage over his fellows. As a result, he will leave more offspring, and the trait will get passed on to later generations. In a sense, natural selection sifts among the variations, excluding some, favoring others. But this is not a conscious choice. With natural selection, Darwin wanted to describe a blind, purposeless process—*without any guidance or planning*—as a way to dispense with design, at least in biology. When Darwinists refer to mutations as random, they mean that these changes are not directed for a purpose.

Evolution, understood in this way, is the best story that materialists have devised for explaining, or explaining away, the exquisite designs of living creatures. They insist that the design of life is an illusion.

We can distill the Darwinian evolutionary story into three basic parts: common ancestry, random mutations, and natural selection. Common ancestry (or common descent) is the idea that all living things trace back, ultimately, to one or a few common ancestors.

When biologists speak or write about evolution, they often combine the three parts of the theory—common descent, natural selection, and random mutations. But they really should be treated separately. For example, a research paper on fossils may purport to show that whales are descended from a species of land mammal. While this evidence *may* count as evidence for common ancestry, it does not and cannot show that random mutations combined with natural selection can account for the transition from land mammals to whales. In other words, even the best evidence of common ancestry isn't evidence for how such a descent occurred.

Before we move on

+ What is the difference between evolution in a general sense and Darwinian evolution? What is one difference between Darwin's theories and today's Neo-Darwinism?

+ What makes natural selection a good fit for a materialistic worldview? How do random mutations fit into a materialist's understanding of natural selection?

+ What is common ancestry? How does it relate to natural selection and random mutation?

THEISTIC EVOLUTION

Some scientists have thought that organisms shared a common ancestor and have slowly changed from one form to another. But unlike Darwin, they have argued that this process was purposefully guided. This was the view of Alfred Russel Wallace, who codiscovered the concept of natural selection at the same time as Charles Darwin. Wallace recognized that natural selection could explain some things; but the longer he studied the natural world, the more convinced he became that only purpose could fully explain it. At the turn of the twentieth century, he defended what we might call an intelligent-design or *teleological* version of evolution. (*Teleological* means "purposeful.")

Others have taken a view like Wallace's, but have argued that while some organisms share a common ancestor, they trace back to separate, original forms, which were perhaps created by God. God in this view sometimes acts directly in the course of nature, and other times guides an otherwise natural process. We could call this view *progressive creationism.*

These days, however, to suggest that evolution might be purposeful can keep an otherwise promising scientist from getting tenure, or getting ahead. Most theistic evolutionists are convinced by the evidence for Darwinism or find it difficult to challenge the consensus, but they don't want to take God completely out of the picture.

But for a clear thinker, this is a tough bullet to bite. After all, if the Darwinian process is *unguided and purposeless*, what sense does it make to say that God guided it? Not much. To say that God guided an unguided process is obvious nonsense.

Besides this troubling logical problem, Christian theistic evolutionists (or rather, theistic Darwinists) have trouble squaring their views with basic Christian beliefs. Were Adam and Eve the first humans from whom we are all descended? Was there a fall into sin at some point in the past? Was God directly involved in the history of life? Did he intend to create human beings? Did he know each of us before we were formed in our mother's womb? If you accept Darwinism, these questions are hard to answer from a Christian perspective. So it's no surprise that prominent theistic evolutionists seek to reinterpret these ideas to reconcile them with Darwinian orthodoxy.

BEFORE WE MOVE ON

+ What is the difference between Darwinian evolution and teleological evolution? What is the difference between Darwinian evolution and progressive creationism?

+ What are some problems theistic evolutionists may encounter as they read the Bible?

INTELLIGENT DESIGN

The idea of intelligent design (ID) doesn't fit neatly on the spectrum of creationists and evolutionists, but it is easy to define. ID is the search for intelligent patterns within nature. The leading ID proponents would agree with the following definition: "ID holds that certain aspects of the universe, such as cosmological fine-tuning and nanomachines inside cells, are best explained by intelligent causes."

Notice that ID does not rely on biblical texts or even say that God is the designer. ID arguments focus simply on the telltale effects of intelligent causes in nature. While creationism begins with the Bible and seeks to confirm God's creative acts using the tools of science, ID begins with an open mind and the evidence from nature and seeks to answer the question: "What is the best explanation for the things we observe?"

ID is compatible with several versions of biological evolution. ID proponents recognize that natural selection explains some things we see in nature, but reject the Darwinian claim that life is entirely the result of purposeless processes and argue that the biological world is filled with evidence of ID. As a result, ID parts company with those theistic evolutionists who seek to make peace with Darwinism.

ID is often mischaracterized by academics, journalists, and opinion makers as "stealth creationism" or "creationism in a cheap tuxedo," repackaged to get around existing laws that prohibit the teaching of creationism in public-school science classrooms. This assertion is false.

Of course, evidence of ID may *point* to God, even though ID arguments don't assume God's existence. Biblical texts such as Psalm 19:1 and Romans 1:20 teach that nature points to God, so as Christians we should expect to find evidence of design, although we shouldn't expect to learn everything about God by studying nature. Traditionally, theologians have regarded the natural world as God's *general* revelation of himself as Creator. Everyone at every time and place has some access to this general revelation. But God has also revealed himself in history and in Scripture. These are his *special* revelations. In our opinion, the evidence of ID, combined with certain philosophical arguments, can provide a strong argument for the existence of a Creator; but it can't tell us God's name, or reveal that God became incarnate as Jesus, or inform us that Jesus died for our sins and was raised from the dead. To know these things, we need special revelation.

BEFORE WE MOVE ON

+ What makes intelligent design (ID) different from creationism and evolution? What makes it different from theistic evolution?

+ What makes the ID approach compatible with—and complementary to—Christianity?

THE LIMITS OF DARWINISM

To the outside observer, the debates over creationism, evolution, and ID can be confusing. Dip into the literature and before long you'll encounter technical terms such as *epigenetics, horizontal gene transfer, genetic drift, gene duplication, planetary habitability*, and *irreducible complexity*. An entry on a pro-Darwinism blog might include a dozen citations to the scientific literature, and a response on a pro-ID blog might contain a dozen more. You might be tempted to just throw up your hands and say something like this: "Maybe evolution is just God's way of creating." But we hope we've convinced you that the issues are too important to avoid with a vague catchphrase. You do need to learn some of the technical jargon to follow the debate closely, but you can learn to recognize the major fault lines without memorizing the dictionary ahead of time.

Darwinists attribute vast creative power to natural selection acting on random mutations, so we should keep most of our attention focused on this key idea. It's easy to lose sight of it because *evolution* refers to so many different kinds of evidence. The edifice of Darwinism rests, in part, on evidence from the fossil record, patterns of similarity in living things, and laboratory and field experiments. If you disentangle these separate threads, you discover that most of the claims for natural selection and random mutations rest not on hard, relevant evidence, but on the assumption that the theory must be true because the main alternative is "unscientific."

The fossil record suggests that life has changed over long periods, but it tells us *nothing* about how those changes took place. And when we turn to laboratory experiments and field observations to test the power of selection and mutation, we find that it explains only tiny changes within species, many of which are cyclical. The few changes that go in one direction almost always involve some loss of function. For example, there are animals living in dark caves that are blind and lack skin coloration. Otherwise, they are much like their relatives in the sunlit world outside. It's reasonable to infer that these animals have lost their eyes and pigment as the result of mutations, which were preserved because it's advantageous not to have eyes or skin pigment in dark caves. But evidence of how eyes can be lost in quirky dark environments doesn't tell us where eyes came from in the first place.

The belief that Darwinian processes can create new biological structures and functions contradicts practically everything we've learned in the century and a half since Darwin proposed his theory. We've found evidence only of trivial, *microevolutionary* changes, never of the *macroevolutionary* changes required by the theory.

For instance, in the longest-running laboratory experiment on bacterial evolution, Richard Lenski and his research teams at Michigan State University have monitored over fifty thousand generations of bacteria. Every mutation they've observed has produced either a slight modification of existing function or loss of function in the bacteria. There has never been a true gain in function, let alone a new system. And despite plenty of laboratory prodding, the bacteria refuse to become anything but the same species of bacteria that was present at the start of the experiment.

Now, if the Darwinian process can't produce new functions in an organism with such an enormous population size and short generation time, then why think that it can make birds, mammals, and fish from simpler creatures?

In his book *The Edge of Evolution: The Search for the Limits of Darwinism*,[1] biochemist Michael Behe seeks out the natural limits to the Darwinian mechanism by studying the history of different organisms—including the parasite that causes malaria, as well as the human response to that parasite, the human immunodeficiency virus, and deadly strains of the *E. coli* bacteria. He shows that Darwin's process can preserve errors that happen to give organisms an advantage, but that it can't do what Darwin imagined it could.

For instance, Behe describes a mutation in some humans that affects the hemoglobin molecules in their red blood cells. People inherit one copy of the gene for hemoglobin from each parent, and if a person inherits the mutant gene from both parents, then the mutant hemoglobin in his or her red cells (which are normally round) will cause those cells to be shaped like a crescent or sickle. Such cells get stuck in blood vessels, and the person suffers from a serous disease called "sickle cell anemia." On the other hand, a person who receives the mutant gene from only one parent is said to have the "sickle cell trait" but can live a normal and healthy life. One might expect natural selection to have eliminated the mutation from human populations, but it turns out that the sickle cell trait helps to protect young children from malaria. The malaria parasite, which is transmitted by mosquitoes and reproduces in human red blood cells, does not do well in cells with one copy of the mutant gene. So although people with two copies of the mutant gene are very sick, those with only one copy tend to be healthier than people with normal hemoglobin in malaria regions such as Africa. As a result, natural selection tends to preserve this mutation over generations.

That's a perfect illustration of the power, and the stark limits, of the Darwinian process. Behe compares it to a city that is besieged by enemy troops. Imagine, for instance, Manhattan Island, which is connected to the nearby mainland by bridges and tunnels. Manhattanites depend on these bridges and tunnels to get around. If a vicious army were about to invade Manhattan, however, New Yorkers might blow up the tunnels and bridges as a last resort to stop the invasion. But no one would imagine that this is a way to build cities, bridges, and tunnels in the first place. In the same way, natural selection can sometimes preserve damaging mutations that provide a narrow advantage to an organism, but such desperate measures reveal little or nothing about where the organisms and their various organs and systems came from in the first place.

Certain regions of DNA contain information needed to build proteins (and much more besides). Proteins are large molecules with complex three-dimensional structure that provide structure and undergo all manner of reactions inside cells. They are involved in thousands of essential cellular processes, including the decoding of the information in DNA to build proteins. The function of a protein depends on its precise shape. The problem for Darwinism is that mutations that improve protein function are very rare. Even worse, certain mutations need to occur in the right order to have the desired functional changes in a protein.

Research conducted by Doug Axe and Ann Gauger of the Biologic Institute shows that even in a universe of vast size and age, the Darwinian process is very unlikely to produce a protein with a new function, even when starting with a protein that is structurally very similar to the target protein. And that's just *one protein*. When thousands of interacting proteins are in view, the prospects for Darwinism are nil.

Before we move on

+ What makes it difficult to keep up with debates between creationists, evolutionists, and ID theorists? What do we need to keep sight of in the midst of the debate?

+ What is characteristic of the changes scientists have observed within species? How does this pose a difficulty for macroevolutionary theory?

+ How is sickle cell mutation a perfect illustration of the Darwinian process overall?

+ How common are mutations that improve protein functions? How common are mutations that produce *new* protein functions?

THE ORIGIN OF LIFE

Of course, even if natural selection acting on random genetic mutations could create new proteins, organs, and animals, it can't account for the origin of life itself. The starting point of Darwinism is with a reproducing population of some kind. Materialists who believe that the physical universe is all there is assume that life somehow evolved from nonlife. In particular, they assume that the biological world bubbled up, somehow, from nonliving chemicals. This is often called *chemical evolution*.

In this spirit, scientists have proposed many naturalistic scenarios for the origin of the first life. All the scenarios are speculative and treat only a fraction of the required steps to get from nonlife to life. Every prominent scientist working in the field has his or her own pet theory, and other prominent scientists in the field criticize it. For a review of recent origin-of-life theories and why they fail, see *Signature in the Cell: DNA and the Evidence for Intelligent Design* by Stephen C. Meyer.[2] As Meyer explains, the dilemma confronting everyone who wants to explain life from mere chemistry is that life is, from top to bottom, an information-rich reality that transcends chemistry.

Even to begin to understand how hard it would be to get life from mere chemicals, we have to simplify the problem—a lot. Meyer does that by focusing mainly on the regions of a DNA molecule, inside the nuclei of cells within organisms, that contain at least some of the information that cells use to produce proteins.

These regions of DNA contain something called complex specified information (CSI), which is encoded in a line like the letters in a book that form meaningful text when arranged in the right order. For instance, imagine a garden with begonias that have been arranged so that they form a pattern that looks exactly like this: "THIS IS A FLOWER GARDEN." How do you know that these flowers were *intentionally* arranged to form this sentence, rather than being randomly scattered by the wind? How do you know that something more than mere gravity, or the ordinary way begonias grow, is involved? You might want to say that it's because they form a complex and improbable pattern. That's part of the story. But it can't be the whole story, because almost *any* pattern would have been improbable. If you just scattered the seeds randomly, and let them grow, the arrangement would be improbable—you'd have a very hard time producing the pattern a second time. So complexity or improbability alone is not a reliable sign of design.

The pattern of flowers forming an English sentence is not just complex (or improbable, which is more or less the same thing), but also independently *specified*. In this case, the pattern is specified by the rules of English grammar and spelling, and is not determined by the way plants grow in soil. Since we know how to read English, we recognize that this is an intelligent pattern. According to ID theorist William Dembski, when a pattern exhibits high amounts of such *specified complexity*, it reliably indicates ID.

In fact, the only known sources for producing large amounts of specified complexity are intelligent agents. That's why ID is a much better explanation for the flower pattern than either chance or a blind process that produces the same simple pattern over and over.

Why is this relevant to our discussion? Because the coding regions of DNA contain the same kind of information as a written text. Of course, rather than English sentences, these regions of DNA give information that cells use to produce functional proteins. Life is far more than DNA, of course; but if you're going to explain life, you have to explain where this information (and much more besides) came from.

Appealing to chemistry to explain this information is like appealing to the properties of ink and paper to explain *Moby Dick*. And we assure you that we are exponentially simplifying the problem for the materialist. This problem besets not just the origin of life, but also the major so-called transitions in the fossil record, such as the Cambrian explosion, when about forty different kinds of animals appear suddenly in the fossil record. It's one thing to draw a line of descent from one organism in the fossil record to another, but it is quite another to account for the origin of new information across time. The long age and vast size of the universe is dwarfed by the information problem.

BEFORE WE MOVE ON

+ What is chemical evolution? Why is it necessary for bio-logical evolution?

+ What is the difference between complex information and specified information? How do both kinds of information play a part in DNA?

+ How does specified complexity point toward ID? What is the "information problem" in chemical evolution?

ID IN COSMOLOGY, PHYSICS, AND ASTRONOMY

The evidences for ID and against materialism are not restricted to biology. A century ago, many scientists believed that the physical universe was eternal. Some were so wedded to this belief that they refused to accept that the question of a beginning was even scientific! And yet, about the time that the Scopes Monkey Trial was taking place in Tennessee (in the 1920s), astronomers such as Edwin Hubble were uncovering evidence that the universe had a beginning. By studying the light from distant galaxies, Hubble found evidence that the entire universe was expanding. This suggested that the universe had a beginning in the finite past. Rather than being eternal, our universe has an age! This gave rise to a new field of science called *cosmology*, which studies the features of the universe as a whole.

At first, some scientists resisted the idea that the universe had a beginning. Motivated by his atheistic beliefs, Fred Hoyle proposed a model of the universe called *Steady State* in 1948 to try to salvage an eternal past. He ridiculed the alternative by refer-ring to it as the *Big Bang* theory—a very misleading name. Over the next decade he managed to win over most astronomers to his side. By the mid-1960s, however, scientists had discovered the Cosmic Microwave Background Radiation. Since this was a major prediction of the Big Bang theory, it effectively killed Hoyle's Steady State theory. Since then, scientists have found several other confirmations of the idea that Hoyle found so troubling.

Since anything that *begins* to exist must have a cause other than itself, we can now be confident that the universe must have a transcendent cause. The material universe, in other words, cannot explain itself. That spells doom for materialism.

In the second half of the twentieth century, physicists also began to realize that many of the properties of the universe seem to be "fine-tuned" for life. This includes the conditions that must have existed at the very beginning—called cosmic initial conditions—as well as physical constants and laws. The most familiar ones are the force of gravity that holds matter together at large scales, and the electromagnetic force that holds atoms together. Change one of these, or many others, by just a tiny fraction and the universe would be uninhabitable. It's as if a vastly complex combination for producing a habitable universe has been initially set. This is powerful evidence that the universe is designed for life.

As it happens, the universe looks designed not only for life but for scientific discovery as well. In *The Privileged Planet: How Our Place in the Cosmos Is Designed for Discovery*,[3] we give examples showing that the same rare places in the universe that allow for complex life are also the best places for observing and discovering the secrets of the universe.

For example, the composition of our atmosphere, the presence of a large moon, our orbit around a yellow middle-aged star, our location in the Milky Way galaxy, and the age of the universe are all important for life. Change these just a little bit and complex life would have a much harder time surviving on our planet. What's surprising is that those same changes would also make it much harder for us to do science. It appears that the universe was set up to allow its intelligent inhabitants to discover the world around them. This doesn't prove God's existence, but it certainly fits comfortably with the Christian idea that nature is one of God's revelations.

Before we move on

+ The field of science known as *cosmology* arose from what discovery in the early 1900s? What common belief did this discovery challenge?

+ What is the difference between the Big Bang theory and the Steady State theory? What about the Big Bang theory spells doom for materialism, and why?

+ What are a few factors that make the universe habitable? What are a few factors that make our planet habitable?

GOD OF THE GAPS AND OTHER COMPLAINTS

Both creationists and ID proponents are often accused of committing the "God-of-the-gaps" fallacy. Supposedly, as our scientific knowledge increases, "natural" explanations have replaced supernatural explanations of the universe. As we discover more about nature, God is called in to fill in ever-smaller gaps of ignorance. Eventually, the need for God will disappear as the few remaining gaps are filled in by natural causes. Or so the argument goes.

This criticism is as common as it is mistaken. It's true that pagans sometimes appealed to supernatural beings, such as Zeus or Thor, to explain lightning, earthquakes, and the like. But there are few well-documented cases of a scientist invoking God to explain a phenomenon that was later explained by physical laws. In the history of science, there may be one clear case of a God-of-the-gaps argument: when Isaac Newton seemed to have invoked God's direct action to account for the stability of

the orbits of the planets around the sun. Later scientists con-
cluded that this was not necessary. But such a case was clearly
the exception rather than the rule. In fact, many historians of
science argue that Christian belief in a rational Creator encour-
aged early scientists to look for regular natural laws to explain
much of what they saw in nature.

It's not as though natural laws were an *alternative* to God—or
to ID, for that matter. As we've seen, the fine-tuning of physical
laws and constants is one of the best pieces of evidence *for* ID in
nature. Sure, we shouldn't prematurely appeal to God's direct
action, or to ID, to explain the things we don't understand. That's
a mere argument from ignorance. But we also shouldn't assume
that the laws of physics and chemistry, and processes such as
natural selection and random mutations, account for *everything*
we find in nature. We should look at the evidence and consider
all the options, including design. Otherwise, we'll be in danger
of a "materialism-of-the-gaps" fallacy, which excludes ID from
science, even when it is the best explanation.

At the same time, according to Christian theology, God does
sometimes act directly in the course of nature, rather than through
natural laws or other causes. God became incarnate in the womb
of a virgin, and raised Jesus from the dead. During his earthly
ministry, Jesus turned water into wine, raised Lazarus from the
dead, and multiplied fishes and loaves. Any Christian concept of
God must accommodate, rather than explain away, such miracles.

Behind the God-of-the-gaps criticism is another idea, often
called *methodological naturalism*. According to methodological
naturalism, all *scientific* explanations must be naturalistic. This
turns science into the search for the best naturalistic explanation
of nature, and excludes ahead of time the very possibility of ID.
But there are already specialized sciences that appeal to intelligent agency, such as archaeology, cryptography, forensics, and

the Search for Extraterrestrial Intelligence (SETI). Why forbid this sort of explanation in science elsewhere?

For instance, imagine that 540 million years ago various forms of animal life were purposely altered so that they could evolve into much more complex animals over the next few million years. A committed methodological naturalist would be unable to give the correct explanation of the event. The ID theorist, in contrast, is open to the possibility that an intelligent agent might explain some fossil evidence. In other words, strict methodological naturalism can lead scientists into error and blind them to important discoveries.

Do we have to know how an intelligent agent produced a pattern or artifact to conclude that design is the best explanation for it? Not at all. Certain patterns can betray the work of ID, even if we don't have all the details. For example, we would not need to know precisely how our hypothetical aliens altered animal life on Earth to accelerate its evolution 540 million years ago in order to detect the effects of their action. And we could detect an intelligent radio signal from an extraterrestrial source, even if we had no other details.

In fact, many important discoveries in science have been made without understanding the mechanisms behind them. Johannes Kepler discovered his three laws of planetary motion by carefully examining the behavior of the planets in the sky. But it took Isaac Newton to explain them in terms of his laws of gravity and motion decades later—and not even Newton understood exactly what gravity is, only what it does. A century ago, Alfred Wegener presented evidence for the idea that the continents were once together and drifted apart, but most geologists rejected it at the time, in part because he did not give a mechanism for how the drift was supposed to happen. In 2011, the three cosmologists who discovered evidence for the acceleration of the universe

CREATION, EVOLUTION, AND INTELLIGENT DESIGN

(dubbed *dark energy*) were awarded the Nobel Prize in physics, even though they have no idea why this happens.

BEFORE WE MOVE ON

+ What is a major problem with the "God-of-the-gaps" view? What is "materialism-of-the-gaps," and why is it also problematic?
+ What are a few flaws in methodological naturalism?
+ Why is it not always necessary to understand mechanisms in order to make important scientific discoveries?

BOTH NEGATIVE AND POSITIVE

OK. But aren't arguments for design just negative arguments? In other words, aren't ID proponents just saying, "I can't think of a naturalistic process to explain this pattern, so I'll just give up and invoke a designer"? No. There's nothing wrong with a negative argument that shows, say, the problems with Darwinism. But most ID arguments go further than that.

Consider the argument that Michael Behe makes in his book *Darwin's Black Box*.[4] Behe focuses on several "molecular machines," such as the blood-clotting cascade and the flagellum, which is a sort of motor that some bacteria use to get around. When he discusses the bacterial flagellum, he evaluates the powers and limits of regular, physical laws and of the Darwinian process. He concludes that these processes probably don't have the power, by themselves, to produce the bacterial flagellum. That's because the locomotive function of the flagellum is inaccessible to the cumulative power of natural selection acting on random mutations. It is, as Behe says, "irreducibly complex." It needs many separate parts working together before it gets the survival-benefiting function. That's the negative part of his argument.

To get a working flagellum, Behe argues, you almost surely need foresight—the exclusive jurisdiction of intelligent agents. That's the positive part of his argument. An agent can produce a system for a future purpose, for an end.

Now, when Behe argues that the tiny molecular machines in cells display evidence of design, he is not just saying that the Darwinian process is very unlikely to produce them. He is also arguing that these systems exhibit just the properties that intelligent agents produce. Whatever produced them needed foresight, since they don't provide the organism with a survival-enhancing function until many of their interacting parts are all put together and in the right way. Natural selection can select only for current function. It can't hold parts in reserve for millions of years until it gets whatever else it needs. Natural selection can't plan for a future function. An intelligent agent can.

BEFORE WE MOVE ON

✤ What is a negative argument for ID? What is a positive argument for ID? What makes the argument positive?

WHO DESIGNED THE DESIGNER?

Suppose you explain all this evidence for ID to your Darwinist friend. Instead of grappling with the evidence, though, he just responds, "Oh, yeah—well, then, who designed the designer?" He thinks he's backed you into a corner, but he's mistaken. You can explain the cause of an event without explaining the cause of the cause. So you can respond, "I don't first have to determine who designed you to conclude that your spoken words were the product of a rational mind with intention and reason." We detect design all the time, without first determining who designed the designer.

That said, there is the question of the first cause—that eternal reality from which everything else derives. Every developed worldview has some answer to the question of the first cause. If God exists, then he is the first cause—that fundamental reality on which everything else depends. Materialists think that something like the material universe is fundamental. Although we can't develop the argument in detail here, our knowledge of cosmic history, in which our universe has a specific age, makes it very difficult to maintain that matter or the material universe is the fundamental reality; but it is quite consistent with the biblical claim that in the beginning, God created the heavens and the earth, that is, everything other than God.

BEFORE WE MOVE ON

+ What is a fundamental reality? Is it necessary to explain the cause of a fundamental reality in order to explain its nature? Why or why not?

IS ID BAD THEOLOGY?

Some critics argue that ID implies that God is a "clumsy tinkerer" who has to keep intervening in nature because he couldn't get it right the first time. But ID is not a theory about how God acts in the world. ID researchers focus on ID's effects in the world, not how those effects come about.

Of course, according to *Christian theology*, God is free to act in all sorts of ways. As we've already discussed, he can act directly, such as when he created the world from nothing. He can also act directly *within* nature without an intermediary, such as when Jesus changed water into wine. And God can act through so-called secondary causes, such as natural laws or even the free choices of human beings. ID is not in itself theology. Thinking of ID from a Christian perspective, however, we would say that ID encourages the investigator to look at the natural world to find out what God has done, rather than dictating ahead of time what he must have done.

If God acted directly in natural history, say, at the origin of life, that would fit perfectly well with the Christian faith. God can do what he wants. Why assume that if God acts directly in nature, he could do so only as an incompetent tinker? We have no reason to *assume* that God wanted to create a world that could do all its own creating. Maybe God is not like a watchmaker seeking to create the perfect self-winding clock. As we suggested earlier, perhaps he's more like a gardener who not only tends his garden, but also creates his own soil, seeds, water, and sun. Perhaps God delights in every moment. Perhaps even an event that we think is the result of natural law is not, as G. K. Chesterton once put it, "a mere recurrence" but "a theatrical encore."[5]

A virtue of ID is that it doesn't require detailed assumptions about when and why God acts. It focuses on public evidence of design that anyone can consider, whatever their beliefs. In fact, an ID theorist need not assume that God exists, but only that it's possible to find evidence for design in nature. In contrast, Darwinists and materialists *assume* that there is no evidence for design in nature and that nature must have created itself.

Just as a square peg is not obliged to conform to a round hole, so nature is not obliged to conform to our expectations. The history of science is replete with examples of discoveries that contradicted widely held beliefs. If God exists and created the universe with real evidence of design, then materialism—methodological or otherwise—is a set of blinders rather than a telescope for discovering the world around us. The rational choice is to be open to evidence of design wherever it may be found, especially since strong evidence of design is already at hand.

BEFORE WE MOVE ON

+ What assumptions are made by materialists? What assumptions are not made by ID theorists? What assumptions should Christians be careful not to make?

WHOM SHOULD YOU TRUST?

People have always looked to authorities to tell them the truth on matters that they know little about. In recent decades, scientists have assumed the authority to explain the natural world. Unfortunately, as a result, some ideas from science are defended not on the basis of evidence, but because they are allegedly supported by a consensus—that is, widespread agreement—among scientists. The suggestion is that everyone is therefore obligated to accept it.

Science is a valuable tool for learning about the natural world, but science is not the only way of knowing. Moreover, scientists are fallen human beings, just like everyone else, so they make mistakes. That's why we have to do our best to figure out when a scientific consensus is based on solid evidence and sound reasoning, and when it is based on social pressure and groupthink.

Anyone who has studied the history of science knows that scientists are not immune to "herd instinct." Many false ideas enjoyed consensus opinion at one time. Indeed, a popular theory can often shape the thinking of scientists so strongly that they are unable to accurately summarize, let alone evaluate, real alternatives. Question the consensus, and some respond with dogmatic fanaticism.

Nevertheless, major advances in science often come from a lone scientist going against the consensus view of the day. These pioneering scientists often endanger their careers for defending their views. A recent example is Dan Shechtman, who won the

Nobel Prize in chemistry in 2011 for discovering a new crystal-line chemical structure. Associated Press reporter Aron Heller wrote that Dr. Shechtman's "colleagues mocked him, insulted him and exiled him from his research group."[6] Other examples are Alfred Wegener's continental-drift theory, Cecilia Payne-Gaposchkin's discovery that the sun consists mainly of hydrogen, and Barry Marshall's discovery that ulcers are caused by a type of bacterium. In the end, the evidence of nature prevailed over the prejudices of the consensus.

The lesson is clear. Be skeptical of claims of consensus, especially when there are big political or metaphysical issues at stake. Ask tough questions. Insist on clear definitions. Educate yourself, using multiple sources of information. Do your best to follow the evidence where it leads. And rest assured that the real evidence of science, as opposed to the misleading claims of scientific materialism, will not conflict with the truths of the Christian faith.

In conclusion

+ What can we learn from the way major scientific advances are often made?
+ Why should we be mindful of the difference between natural science and scientific naturalism? Why is one compatible with Christianity? Why is the other not?
+ What advice do the authors give for entering into the debate? What makes each piece of advice so important?

FOR FURTHER READING

Behe, Michael. *Darwin's Black Box*. New York: Free Press, 1996.

_____. *The Edge of Evolution: The Search for the Limits of Darwinism*. New York: Free Press, 2007.

Collins, C. John. *Science and Faith: Friends or Foes?* Wheaton, IL: Crossway Books, 2003.

Gonzalez, Guillermo, and Jay W. Richards, *The Privileged Planet: How Our Place in the Cosmos Is Designed for Discovery.* Washington, DC: Regnery Publishing, 2004.

Meyer, Stephen C. *Darwin's Doubt: The Explosive Origin of Animal Life and the Case for Intelligent Design.* San Francisco: HarperOne, 2013.

_____. *Signature in the Cell: DNA and the Evidence for Intelligent Design.* San Francisco: HarperOne, 2009.

Richards, Jay W., editor. *God and Evolution: Protestants, Catholics, and Jews Explore Darwin's Challenge to Faith.* Seattle: Discovery Institute Press, 2010.

NOTES

1. New York: Free Press, 2007.
2. New York: HarperOne, 2009.
3. Washington, DC: Regnery Publishing, 2004.
4. New York: Free Press, 1996.
5. *Orthodoxy*, chap. 4, available at http://www.leaderu.com/cyber/books/orthodoxy/ch4/html.
6. Aron Heller, "Vindicated: Ridiculed Israeli Scientist Wins Nobel," Associated Press, October 5, 2011, http://news.yahoo.com/vindicated-israeli-scientist-wins-nobel-183256852.html.